FLORIDA *Saturdays*

At the Swamp

AN INSIDE LOOK AT THE PAGEANTRY, TRADITION
AND SPIRIT OF GAME DAY AT THE UNIVERSITY OF FLORIDA

TEXT BY
DAVID STIRT

PHOTOS BY
GLENN DANFORTH

FOREWORD BY
DANNY WUERFFEL

SP
SPORTS
PUBLISHING
L.L.C.

www.SportsPublishingLLC.com

ISBN: 1-58261-113-0

PUBLISHER
Peter L. Bannon

SENIOR MANAGING EDITOR
Susan M. Moyer

ACQUISITIONS EDITOR
John Humenik

DEVELOPMENTAL EDITOR
Dean Miller

PHOTO EDITOR
Erin Linden-Levy

BOOK DESIGN
Heidi Norsen

COPY EDITOR
Cindy McNew

ART DIRECTOR
K. Jeffrey Higgerson

COVER DESIGN
Kenneth O'Brien

DUST JACKET DESIGN
Heidi Norsen

PHOTO IMAGING
Kerri Baker
Dustin Hubbart
Christine Mohrbacher
Heidi Norsen

MEDIA AND PROMOTIONS MANAGER
Jonathan Patterson, Regional Marketing Mgr.
Randy Fouts, National Marketing Mgr.
Maurey Williamson, Print Marketing Mgr.

Printed in the United States of America

Sports Publishing L.L.C.
804 North Neil Street
Champaign, IL 61820

Phone: 1-877-424-2665
Fax: 217-363-2073
Web site: www.SportsPublishingLLC.com

To Jill, Ben and Danny, all of whom have enjoyed The Swamp experience, but also have brought more joy to my life than any football game ever has or ever will.

David Stirt

Acknowledgments
By David Stirt

After watching Gator football games at Florida Field for 25 years, first as a graduate student at UF, as a reporter for many years, then as a fan for five years and most recently as the publisher of *Fightin' Gators* magazine, I've had plenty of chances to observe most of the game-day traditions that are detailed in this book. Those observations served as my reference points when John Humenik asked me whether I'd be interested in trying to verbalize the experiences of a day at The Swamp, providing words that would help **enliven the visual memories** stimulated by Glenn Danforth's wonderful set of photos.

In order to try to bring the game-day traditions to life, I needed to go to the sources of those traditions. As any writer will tell you, great storytellers, with great stories to tell, make the experience not only enlightening, but a joy as well. I was lucky enough to be able to speak with a group of people with great stories to tell who were willing to share those stories with me.

Before I pursued the individuals, and the various **game-day rituals and traditions** they are a part of, I knew I had to start with the acknowledged historian of all things Gator football—Norm Carlson. Thanks to Norm's memory, and guidance, I was able to head in the right directions to find the source material that helped shape this book.

A special thanks to George Edmondson, Stumpy Harris, Richard Johnston, Chip Howard and Mark Sexton for giving me so much of their time and so many wonderful stories. And a heartfelt thank-you to Marion Finch, the widow of longtime stadium p.a. announcer Jim Finch, who was kind enough to welcome me into her home and share her memories of Jim, not an easy thing to do so soon after his passing.

Research into the history of Florida Field and many of the game-day traditions would have been an arduous task without the aid of Carl Van Ness, the curator of manuscripts and archives at the University of Florida. Carl not only pulled together key files for me but also led me to other archival material from which I was able to piece together the **behind-the-scenes** developments that led to the construction of Florida Field.

I'd also like to thank Dean Miller at Sports Publishing, who had to take over this project in midstream, yet showed me far more patience than I deserved as my search for additional material pushed back the production schedule. And thanks again to John Humenik at Sports Publishing, who in offering me this project, showed a lot of faith in me by believing I could handle the job.

Acknowledgments
By Glenn Danforth

Thank you to the great people from Florida's Sports Information Department, both past and present, who allowed me the rare opportunity to combine my **passions for sports** and photojournalism and to do it where only my wildest dreams once allowed me to roam.

Thank you to my editors, Erin Linden-Levy and Dean Miller, for their help and patience. And a special thank you to John Humenik without whom this book and everything leading up to it would never have been possible. Your faith and friendship have honored me.

To Ray Hines III, a heartfelt thank you for your selfless friendship and support, which was invaluable to me as I worked on this book. Thanks for being there when it was needed most.

And to John Freeman, the heart and soul of the University of Florida photojournalism program, thank you for the friendship and inspiration that has helped many times and in many ways in keeping the shutter "bug" alive and kicking.

And most of all, to the sources of my inspiration, my brother, Todd Danforth, my children, Jeremy, Nicole and Dylan Danforth, and my brother-in-arms, Kevin Tirrell, **I dedicate my work** on this book. I love you all beyond words—so I say it in pictures, too.

Foreword

By Danny Wuerffel

Growing up the son of an Air Force Chaplain, I lived on military bases all over the country, including a few years in Spain. We moved every three years, making it difficult to develop a firm loyalty for any particular team. I was a young, traveling football fan without a team.

In August of 1988, my dad was stationed in Fort Walton Beach, Florida. I quickly learned of the strong passions and deep loyalties of Florida football fans. Their personal allegiance and passion to their team was indeed something to admire.

In the fall of 1990, I took my first trip to Ben Hill Griffin Stadium at Florida Field. I experienced my first Gator Growl and then watched Shane Matthews and the **rest of the Gator squad** soundly defeat the Akron Zips on a beautiful Saturday Homecoming afternoon. I couldn't have imagined that weekend what an instrumental role Florida Field would one day play in my life.

I played my first game on Florida Field in 1991, but it wasn't as a Gator. As a senior at Fort Walton Beach High School, we brought our team and 4,000 fans to Ben Hill Griffin Stadium to play for the state championship. Another bright and sunny afternoon—what I later discovered to be the norm—that **day foreshadowed** many amazing moments that would occur on that same field. We won 39-14, and my performance caught the eye of Florida's up-and-coming coach, Steve Spurrier, who watched from an empty corner of the stadium.

As awe-inspiring as a state champi-
onship game at Florida Field with a couple of thousands of fans could be, I'll never forget the first time
I ran out of the tunnel into "The Swamp" as a Florida
Gator. I found myself engulfed by the deafening noise
and amazing colors, a scene that remains so vivid in my
mind. I had entered a world where the primary colors
were only orange and blue, and the overwhelming support and passion of the faithful fans elevated our spirits and strengthened our determination
week after week. Gator fans would just not let us get
down and in turn, we did not want to let them down.
Their determination and belief that they can and do
make a difference on game day resulted in "The
Swamp" taking on a special aura and gaining a
national reputation as arguably the best home
field advantage in all of college football. That magical
environment created a sincere love affair between the
fans and the players that is truly unique and special.

Over my four-year playing career, the Lord
blessed me with more memorable experiences than any
one person deserves. Looking back over four SEC
Championships, a National Title and a **Heisman
Trophy,** I often pinch myself to be certain I'm not
dreaming. However, at the time I found it difficult to
process and fully appreciate the magnitude of each
moment. I constantly had to focus on the task at
hand. As soon as one game ended, we quickly began
preparation for our next opponent. **Joyful victory**
celebrations never lasted more than a couple of days
there was always more work to be done.

That is why I am so thankful for this
book—it gives me the opportunity to recall the loyal
fan support and incredible atmosphere I and so many
other Gator players experienced at Florida Field. I feel
privileged to have an opportunity to express my grati-
tude to the **Gator Nation** for turning my four wonderful years at "The Swamp" into a lifetime of memories that I will hold dear to my heart forever.

As I review the pictures from *A Season of Saturdays at The Swamp,* I'm flooded with countless memories of a college career that kids can only dream of—yet one that I really lived. But this book is not to be treasured by just former players like me. Join me as this photo essay book helps all Gators to remember the special times in this amazing place, a place that came to be known all around the nation as simply The Swamp, the most magical and electric **game-day atmosphere** in all of college football. I believe that you will also be flooded with memories as you page through this beautiful book and review the superb photos of Glenn Danforth and the insightful words of David Stirt, two longtime journalists who follow the Gators.

All Gator fans know that Florida Field is THE place to be on a college football Saturday. From every corner of the state, Gator fans plan for and treasure the game-day experience throughout the year. Through the pages of this book you will feel all of the tradition, rituals and atmosphere of the Florida Gator football **game-day experience,** an experience unmatched anywhere else in the nation. It will help you relive that experience throughout the year. It will help you and so many others understand once again how fortunate we are at the University of Florida and why it is great to be a Florida Gator.

God Bless you and Go Gators!

Danny Wuerffel was the 1996 Heisman Trophy Recipient at the University of Florida

Introduction

By David Stirt

It usually happens only six times a year, although on two occasions (the 1994 and 2002 seasons), Gator football fans were able to enjoy Nirvana a seventh time. The dates are circled on calendars, with indelible orange or blue ink in many instances, as soon as they are announced. Weddings are moved to Saturdays that won't conflict with these pilgrimages. And indeed, for many of the Florida faithful, they are in their own way, quasi-religious experiences. Football **Saturdays at The Swamp** are indeed something very special.

There are various pockets of intense football interest around America, but it's no mistake that college football has been labeled a religion in the South. Long before professional sports franchises finally made their way below the Mason-Dixon Line, college football had a firm and deeply entrenched foothold as the king of sports. And even now, with pro football teams located in Louisiana, Georgia, North Carolina and Florida, and pro baseball, hockey and basketball teams scattered throughout the South, **no team sport rivals** college football when it comes to fan interest.

The Southeastern Conference has led the nation in total attendance every year since 1980 and in 2003 drew an all-time record 6,146,890 fans to its games. The conference is the home of five of the top eight teams nationally in average attendance per game and seven of the top 13. And in all but one year since 1982, the SEC has led all conferences in stadium capacity percentage.

With its latest expansion, Ben Hill Griffin Stadium at Florida Field became one of seven college stadiums in the country that can seat more than 90,000 fans, and further elevated The Swamp's status as one of America's football meccas.

On those half-dozen weekends each fall when the Gators play football at The Swamp, all roads around the state of Florida lead to that hallowed ground situated just off the corner of University Avenue and North-South Drive in Gainesville. The football game may be the centerpiece event for fans making the trek from Pensacola or Key West, from Jacksonville or Ft. Myers or any number of points in between, but a day at The Swamp has become so much **more than just football.** It's an experience encompassing sights and sounds that create camaraderie and continuity for generations of alumni and fans, both young and old.

Introduction
By Glenn Danforth

The second half was about to start and I was out of position. With dozens of photographers jockeying for primo on-field real estate, outside The Swamp was not where I needed to be. It was time to run.

I bolted out of the tunnel just as the ball left the kicking tee and knelt in a rare, wide-open sideline spot next to Florida State's end zone. With elbow room usually in short supply, I thought it odd to have enough space to park a cement truck, but I wasn't complaining. The kickoff was heading right at me and with nobody near me and my left hand firmly gripping my photo gear, **it seemed fate** had intervened to allow me to live my childhood dream of making a spectacular one-handed catch in front of thousands of America's wildest college football fans.

I hummed the *Sports Center* theme song and reveled in the glory of my catch replaying endlessly on ESPN before reality intervened in the visage of an armored crimson mass approaching at close to Mach one. It was time to run.

Time ran out.

My life flashed before me, but I only made it to third grade before instinct tried to save me from the destiny of a love bug on the Florida Turnpike, making me spin away to protect my precious equipment—and my photo gear too—an instant before the Seminole return man **snagged the ball** and brushed past.

As I cursed the kickoff-stealing glory hog in a dialect I invented on the spot to avoid risking death again so soon, the adrenaline coursing through my veins at about 200 beats per minute gave me a rare moment of clarity. **I suddenly realized** why I hadn't needed to fight a gaggle of surly photographers for my great vantage point—I was standing on the playing field, two feet from the sideline.

As I slithered off the field, trying in vain to project my "I meant to do that" look while wishing myself into a state of invisibility, I wondered how many angles CBS was using to showcase my idiocy to a national audience. **My only hope of escape,** it seemed, rested upon the men with badges and guns who would surely arrive momentarily to escort me from Ben Hill Griffin Stadium.

But the armed escort never came, my media pass wasn't revoked and only a swiftly fading tape of the telecast I stored in a sunny, humid location on a large bed of refrigerator magnets is left to remind me that the difference between one of the planet's coolest jobs and donning a grease-caked name tag every day **to seek the answer** to that age-old question, "Do you want fries with that?" is but a matter of inches; the number of inches my head must travel before dislodging itself from the dark nether region it visits occasionally.

That play, a few seasons past, should have secured my enshrinement in the bonehead hall of fame, but I somehow escaped unscathed and without becoming the answer to a college football trivia quiz question. It was a lesson well-learned. Since then I have somehow managed to stay off the field when the ball is in play and have vastly **improved my record** during breaks in the action. Come to think of it, I haven't clunked anyone in the head with my 14-pound lens in ages, and losing my expensive Compact Flash cards along with the 300 or so digital photos they contain has slowed to almost a trickle.

Learning to concentrate in The Swamp's frenetically charged atmosphere hasn't been easy. Wandering the sidelines, alternately dodging receivers wrapped in a trio of defensive backs and the occasional flying cheerleader is hard enough for those who are there strictly to take pictures, but it's nearly impossible for a football fan with a camera. **I admire those** in my profession who use the time between plays checking their digital handiwork on the backs of their cameras, but to me it reeks of reading a book between plays while watching at home.

There is truly no place like The Swamp. Every crowd is unique and each game offers a fascinating new experience. I don't want to miss a moment.

I will keep working on my concentration skills even if it means eventually sacrificing the "somebody please pinch me" sensation I get every fall Saturday when I first walk out of the tunnel onto Florida Field and realize someone is crazy enough to pay me to be where so many Gator fans would willingly give up a body part to be. I know I'll miss all the great things I see from **such a privileged** perspective and the other-worldly feeling of sharing in Gator triumphs, but at least I probably won't end up scampering down the sideline some day after running on the field to **intercept a Tennessee pass.**

In the end, concentration will probably be a good thing. After all, nothing is as useless as a photographer who can't focus.

SATURDAYS AT THE SWAMP

THE FLORIDA GATORS FOOTBALL EXPERIENCE

John James Tigert probably never imagined that the stadium he first championed in 1928 when he arrived in Gainesville as the University of Florida's third president would someday become one of America's best-known college football venues. Still, when he accepted the presidency of UF and **arrived on campus** in September 1928, he was well aware of college football's growing importance nationally, and Florida's development as a Southern football power.

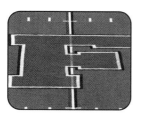  

While at the University of Kentucky as the chairman of the philosophy department in 1919, Tigert served as both head of the athletic department and coach of the football team. His interest in college athletics, and football in particular, continued during his tenure as Commissioner of Education during both the Warren Harding and Calvin Coolidge presidential administrations, so that by the time he came to Florida, he understood the growing popularity of college football and the impact it could have on a university.

Tigert observed that impact in the fall of 1928 when first-year head coach Charles Bachman led the Gators to national prominence with eight **straight wins** before losing their claim to the national championship with a heartbreaking 13-12 loss to Tennessee at Knoxville to close the season. Still, the Gators **finished as the nation's** highest-scoring team with 336 points and drew positive and extensive press notices for themselves and the University with their performance.

While the coincidence of Tigert's arrival at Florida just weeks before the football team embarked on its greatest season might appear to have been the impetus for his plans to construct a stadium with permanent seating to **replace Fleming** Field as the home of the football Gators, in fact, Tigert was discussing ideas for a stadium almost as soon as he became president.

In a letter to Tigert dated November 24, 1928, M.M. Parrish, the Florida state manager for Inter-Southern Life Insurance Company based in Louisville, mentioned earlier discussions he had with Dr. Tigert about stadium plans and detailed a plan being arranged by state representative R.L. Black to introduce **a bill in the Florida Legislature** seeking an appropriation of $150,000 to $200,000 "for the purpose of erecting a first unit of a stadium at the University."

Parrish went on to explain his concept for the new stadium:

"I have thought a good deal about the stadium proposition and my candid judgment, after considering the matter, is that we do not need an expensive, half-million-dollar concrete stadium in this warm climate. A **steel stadium** will serve our needs acceptably and will have the advantage of better ventilation and comfort to the spectators and create better playing conditions for the teams. From the investigation I have made, I believe a steel stadium can be built at a cost not exceeding $5.00 per seat.

"**For $100,000** we could build a stadium on the campus that would seat 20,000 people, and frankly I do not think we will have more than 20,000 people for a **Florida football** game on campus for at least a five-year period from this date."

> "
> *A steel stadium will serve our needs acceptably and will have the advantage of better ventilation and comfort to the spectators and create better playing conditions for the teams. From the investigation I have made, I believe a steel stadium can be built at a cost not exceeding*
> "
> *$5.00 per seat.*

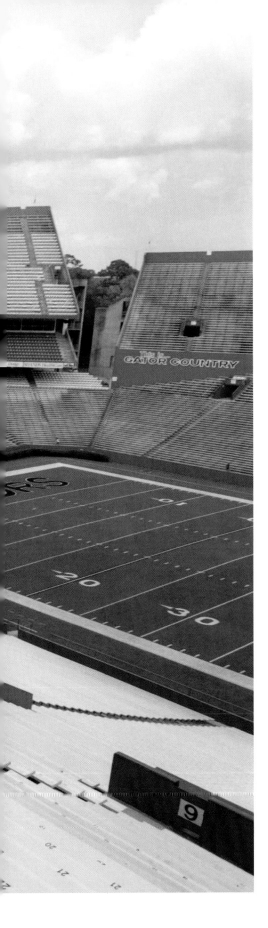

Because the state of Florida faced serious economic problems in the late 1920s due to a collapse in the land boom, a decline in citrus production, a Mediterraean Fruit Fly invasion and a pair of devastating hurricanes in 1926 and 1928, Tigert's administration at Florida began in the midst of a financial crisis that would continue for most of his 20-year tenure. After considering Parrish's proposal, Tigert **replied with a letter** that detailed a spending philosophy for University of Florida athletics that has been followed for more than 75 years.

"I wish to say that I believe an attempt to secure an appropriation out of state funds to build this stadium will be a mistake, and is likely to injure rather than help the University, although I appreciate the desire of Representative Black and others to help," Tigert said in his December 3, 1928 letter to Parrish.

"However, I believe that adequate seating facilities can be properly financed by the Athletic Association, and that it will not be necessary to ask the state to make an appropriation. If an appropriation is made for this purpose, I am sure it will hamper the securing of appropriations for other things, which are needed as badly as a stadium, and for which there is no means of providing, except from state funds. The University **badly needs** recitation rooms, dormitory space and other facilities, which are directly related to the curricula work of the institution.

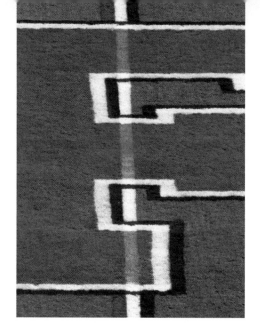

"I am thoroughly in accord with the ideas expressed in your letter with reference to the kind of structure that we should have. A half-million-dollar concrete stadium would certainly be a waste. A steele [sic] stadium, such as you describe, and which may be enlarged with the growth of the institution, and possibly moved, in case of unexpected developments, **appeals to me** strongly. Likewise, I think that a capacity of 20,000 people would meet our requirements for several years. There might be one or two games in the next five years where we would have larger crowds, but these exceptional crowds could be provided for by additional temporary seats."

With the euphoria of the highly successful 1928 football campaign still being felt in the spring of 1929, UF athletic director Everett Yon outlined the need for a football stadium.

"Football can never properly develop until a stadium is built here on the campus, and the project is now underway," Yon wrote. "Large gate receipts in football are necessary to carry on the other branches of sport, and a stadium will enable us to obtain the **increased revenue.** Another great advantage of a stadium will be the bringing of many thousands of people to the campus and making them better acquainted with our university."

> " *There might be one or two games in the next five years where we would have larger crowds, but these exceptional crowds could be provided for by* **"** *additional temporary seats.*

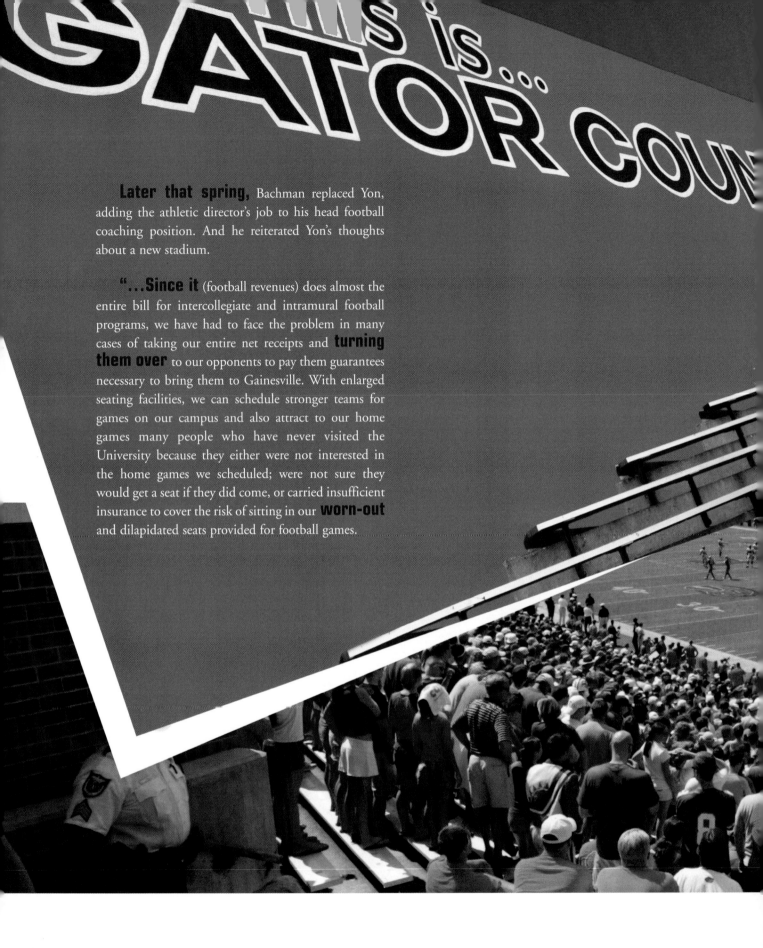

This is... GATOR COUN

Later that spring, Bachman replaced Yon, adding the athletic director's job to his head football coaching position. And he reiterated Yon's thoughts about a new stadium.

"...Since it (football revenues) does almost the entire bill for intercollegiate and intramural football programs, we have had to face the problem in many cases of taking our entire net receipts and **turning them over** to our opponents to pay them guarantees necessary to bring them to Gainesville. With enlarged seating facilities, we can schedule stronger teams for games on our campus and also attract to our home games many people who have never visited the University because they either were not interested in the home games we scheduled; were not sure they would get a seat if they did come, or carried insufficient insurance to cover the risk of sitting in our **worn-out** and dilapidated seats provided for football games.

"**A stadium on the campus** will overcome these objections and will bring to the University people who have never seen the school and therefore do not realize what **a wonderful institution** the state has provided for higher education for her youth. A section to seat in the neighborhood of twelve thousand people, we believe, will be sufficient to provide for our present needs. We hope to have the work **completed in time** for our Homecoming game with Clemson on November 16."

While Bachman's hopes for the completion date of the new stadium turned out to be too optimistic, on April 1, 1929, in a letter to Rudolph Weaver, the dean of Florida's architecture department, Tigert did authorize the preparation of plans for the **new stadium.** A few months later, in his president's page which appeared regularly in the *Florida Alumnus* magazine, Tigert, for the first time in a public forum, discussed his reasons for going forward with the plan for a new stadium.

"...At present it is impossible to play an important game in Gainesville because a large crowd cannot be accommodated here. Playing our games outside Gainesville greatly interferes with the academic work during the fall, necessitates long trips and expense which otherwise **might be avoided,** and complicates a number of things relating to student welfare."

Several years earlier, Tigert had been asked to give his opinion about the value of building a **new stadium** when the University of Nebraska had begun a campaign to do so, and Tigert repeated his comments when addressing the notion of a new stadium for the University of Florida.

"The Stadium was the epitome of the glory that was Greece," Tigert wrote. "Here was displayed the highest expression of the ancient mind and body. Dramatic art, oratory, philosophy, and athletic prowess blended to make the Hellenic civilization the finest of the ancient world. That civilization flowered no less in the exploits of the **Olympic games** than in the oratory of Demosthenes, the philosophy of Aristotle, and the drama of Sophocles. To the Greek the perfection of the physique was no less admirable than the excellence of the mind. The laurel crown of the Olympian victor was as eagerly acclaimed as the prize of the orator, philosopher or dramatist. It was the **stadium that gave** Greek life its symmetry.

"Likewise, the stadium has become the means of unifying the best in American college life. The stadia of Harvard, of Syracuse, of Princeton, the bowl of Yale and the university amphitheatres have made possible the balancing pf physical prowess with intellectual achievement, an exhibition of the best elements of college life, and, above all **that community** of spirit, which is the essence of a great institution and the accomplishment of education in its most complete sense.

"No American university can grow in numbers or in spirit, as it should, without a stadium as an adequate forum for the expression of its community of effort, spirit and activity."

> *" To the Greek the perfection of the physique was no less admirable than the excellence of the mind. The laurel crown of the Olympian victor was as eagerly acclaimed as the prize of the orator, philosopher or dramatist. It was the stadium that gave Greek "*
> *life its symmetry.*

The University of Florida began playing collegiate football in 1906 and from 1908-15 went unbeaten at home, playing its games on Fleming Field, an athletic field named after Francis Fleming Jr., a member of the Florida Board of Control and the son of Florida's 15th governor. The field was used for football, baseball and track and ran north and south with baseball grandstands in the northwest corner of the field. **Bleachers were later extended** along the sidelines, although during football games, fans would park their cars on the sidelines and sit on the hoods to watch.

While the Gators did play five games in Gainesville during the 1925 season, the home schedule featured only three games each in the 1926-28 seasons and only two games in Gainesville in 1929. In both 1927 and 1928, the team played four games in Jacksonville and in 1929 the team played a pair of games in Jacksonville, one in Tampa and another in Miami. The athletic department was getting solid **financial guarantees** for appearing in games away from Gainesville, and it was those gate receipts that put the athletic association in position to pay for the new stadium.

With design plans well underway in late 1929, a site was chosen directly south of Fleming Field for construction of the new stadium. The site was a U-shaped depression, one of many karst sink formations (eroded lime depressions) that dot Florida's landscape. This particular formation included a small spring along its east wall. The **water from the spring** was diverted when the stadium was constructed and now flows through pipes in the east stands.

In the earliest years of the university, the spring's output of pure water was augmented by raw sewage dumped into the depression, creating a bog, or swampy conditions, a fact that became significant in the new nickname for the stadium, which came into vogue some 60 years after its construction. According to Klein Graham, UF's business manager from 1907-48, the sink was dammed at one time and **a duck pond was created** as a supplementary food source for the cafeteria. There was also a hen house on the east bank that supplied meat and eggs.

The stadium architects recognized that the site formed a natural mold for a football stadium, and even though some 55,000 cubic yards of soil had to be removed when construction began in April 1930, the natural depression of the land allowed the stadium to be built below ground level. When fans entered the stadium at what had been ground level before construction began, they were actually on the 32nd row of the stadium, which stood some 25 feet above the playing field. **The playing field** was located approximately three feet below the first row of the newly built concrete seats.

Several months before construction got underway, there was a plea from Frank Wright, the editor of *The Florida Alumnus* magazine, on behalf of football fans who would be attending games at the new stadium, but whose comfort was not being taken into consideration in the stadium design plans. Unlike Fleming Field, which ran north and south, **Wright urged the architects** to lay out the field in an east-west direction.

"**...The tortuous afternoons** spent by those fans who try to see a football game with a blazing sun beaming squarely in their faces cannot be laughed off," Wright wrote. "…If the gridiron was laid out east and west, the great majority of the spectators--- who make football a success—who go further than that— they make all branches of **college athletics** possible—would be afforded the opportunity to receive their money's worth without suffering the agony of combating a **rabid Florida sun.**

"**True, such a move** would impose a hardship upon the football players, but whatever handicap was caused would be equalized. At most each team would have the **sun to face only two** quarters of the game—as it is, the fans must battle Old Sol thru four periods.

"**...the stadium will** have to be paid for from receipts at the gate. Let us think in terms of the mass, since large crowds are the kingpins of football success, and provide them with accommodations and protections that will be appreciated; will be conducive to long continued and more wholesale support than ever before. For cloudy days the old way is all right, but when the **sun shines brightly,** as it does for most of our football games, give us a stadium with the gridiron running east and west."

> **"**
> *For cloudy days the old way is all right, but when the sun shines brightly, as it does for most of our football games, give us a stadium with the gridiron running* **"** *east and west.*

As any Gator fan who has been to Florida Field knows, Wright's plea did nothing to alter the north and south layout plan of the new stadium.

Wright was correct in assuming that gate receipts would factor into the structuring of payments for the construction of the stadium. Heading into the 1929 football season, the athletic association was carrying a $40,000 debt, but with Florida's gate receipts from the 1929 season, including a hefty $35,000 as its share for a game in Atlanta against Georgia Tech which was attended by 44,000 fans, the athletic association had $90,000 on hand in January 1930. After **putting aside money** for spring sports and other past obligations, there remained some $65,000 to put toward stadium construction. The remaining cost would be paid with loans from private sources and the indebtedness was **to be retired** with future stadium receipts.

By the time the football season opened in September 1930, more than 9,000 of the planned 22,000 concrete seats had been poured. While the design of the structure was such that it would be able to accommodate future expansion that could increase the seating capacity to more than 50,000, the initial unit was a complete stadium in its own right, with **30 rows of seats** extending the full length of three sides of the field, with the southern end of the stadium being the only exposed portion of the stadium. Unlike other stadiums built in an oval or horseshoe design, the north endzone area was built on a **straight line to connect** the two sideline sections of the stadium.

At a final cost of $118,000, the stadium not only came in under budget, but at an approximate cost of $5 per seat was less than the projected costs for stadiums at Notre Dame ($12 per seat), Illinois ($30.80 per seat), Pittsburgh ($30 per seat) and Michigan ($11 per seat).

After opening the 1930 season with four wins, the Gators played their final game at Florida Field on October 25, dropping a 14-13 decision to Furman. After a 0-0 tie the following week against Georgia in Savannah, the stage was set for one of the momentous days in University of Florida history.

With Florida governor Doyle Carlton, Alabama governor Bibb Graves, University of Alabama president George Denny and numerous dignitaries from around the state of Florida on hand, the Gators inaugurated their magnificent new stadium on November 8, 1930, with a Homecoming game against national power Alabama.

An overflow crowd of 21, 769 fans attended the festivities, which included a halftime performance by the 70-piece marching band, and Alabama proved to be far too strong for Coach Bachman's Gator squad, shutting out the home team 20-0. Despite the loss, a new era for both the University and its football program had been christened in spectacular fashion.

"Above all we can congratulate ourselves on the completion and dedication of the new stadium which will meet our needs in an adequate way for some years to come," John Tigert wrote in December 1930. "The attendance at the dedicatory game, when some 20,000 came to Gainesville in the rain from all over the state, was a most heartening and stimulating thing and revealed latent support which we did not suspect."

"
   The attendance at the dedica-

tory game, when some 20,000

came to Gainesville in the rain

from all over the state, was a

most heartening and stimulating

thing and revealed latent support
                                    "
which we did not suspect.

The Gators played only two games in their new home in 1931, tying North Carolina 0-0 and losing the Homecoming game to Georgia 33-6, so it wasn't until September 25, 1932, that Florida's first ever win at the new stadium came against The Citadel. Although the stadium wasn't officially dedicated until October 13, 1934, Tigert made it clear before the first game was played in the stadium in 1930 **why Florida Field** was an appropriate name for the structure.

"It has been my hope and desire that the field be **named Florida Field,** after our great state, and that it be dedicated to Florida men who gave their lives in the World War," Tigert wrote. "In this way no personalities are involved, and certainly we can never sufficiently perpetuate the memory of those gallant lads who gave their youth **in the hope that the world** might grow old in peace."

Even though Florida football teams had only four winning seasons during the first 20 years after Florida Field was built, support continued to grow among students, alumni and other **fans of the Gators.** While the seating capacity had been expanded to nearly 26,000 with the addition of 3,900 bleacher seats placed on the east side of the stadium and in the south end zone, it was clear that by the late 1940s, it was time to seriously consider adding on to the existing stadium. Back in 1930 when Florida was built, there were some 2,000 students at the University, but by 1949 that number **had increased** to more than 10,000.

In a proposed financing plan for an addition to Florida Field, it was stated that the students occupied the entire east side of the stadium, including 2,400 bleacher seats and part of the north endzone. Of the remaining 16,000 available seats, a sizeable number had to be allotted to visiting opponents, and at the 1949 Homecoming game, where attendance was 27,347, thousands more fans would have attended if seating had been available. As it was, some of the University's faculty members couldn't even get tickets to the game.

In 1950 Bob Woodruff was hired as the new head football coach and athletic director, replacing Raymond Wolf. **Woodruff insisted** that Florida needed to expand the stadium in order to attract major teams to Gainesville and to be able to play home-and-home series with other Southeastern Conference teams which had larger stadium capacities. The plans were already in the works for an expansion before Woodruff arrived, calling for an additional 11,242 permanent seats and a press box on the west side of the stadium. With the addition of more temporary bleachers on the east side of the stadium, **capacity was doubled** from the original seating of some 22,000 to nearly 44,000 for the final home game of the 1950 season. The University Athletic Association spent $650,000 for the expansion with $150,000 in available funds and the remaining $500,000 supplied through revenue certificates that were paid off with future gate receipts.

It was another 15 years before Florida Field underwent its second expansion, with construction starting on a 10,000-seat addition for the east stands to bring the permanent seating capacity to 56,164. By moving the temporary bleachers into the south endzone, **total stadium capacity** stood at 62,800 for the 1966 season.

Three more stadium expansions followed in the next 27 years. The completion of permanent seating in the south endzone and the addition of skyboxes on top of the west stands pushed capacity to 72,000 in 1982. Nine years later, construction of new seating in the north endzone, including the **Touchdown Terrace** and adjoining suites, increased capacity to 83,000 for the 1991 season, making Florida Field one of the eight largest on-campus stadiums in the country and the largest stadium in the state of Florida.

Ten years later, a $50-million construction project began to expand the press box level, add a new club level with chair backs, renovate existing suites and construct new suites on the west side of the stadium. Two years later, on August 30, 2003, a Florida Field record crowd of 90,011 fans filled the newly expanded stadium.

From the very start, the below-ground-level location of its playing field and **a large segment** of its stands plus the nature of its construction made Florida Field a natural amphitheatre that retained much of the noise generated by fans. By opting not to include a track around the playing field, as was common in many other stadiums, the stands were built very close

to the sidelines and the north endzone. With each expansion, the stadium **became more closed** in, making it easier to retain the noise inside and in turn creating a louder and more hostile environment for visiting teams. By the time Steve Spurrier returned to Florida as the Gator head coach in 1990, the stadium had earned a reputation as one of the **country's loudest** football venues, and that was before the addition of 11,000 seats for the 1991 season.

Prior to the last two expansion projects, Florida Field underwent the first of what would be two name changes, one official, the other unofficial.

At dedication ceremonies on September 9, 1989, the stadium was renamed Ben Hill Griffin Stadium at Florida Field, in honor of Ben Hill Griffin, Jr., a central Florida citrus magnate who had been an extremely generous, longtime benefactor of the University. Only a few months later, Spurrier made his return to Gainesville, and his **immediate success** became the impetus for another renaming of the stadium two years later.

"We had talked about getting a nickname for the stadium because we thought it would help from an exposure standpoint," explained Norm Carlson, UF's sports information director from 1956-2003. "Everything we came up with was tacky. Nothing ever seemed to ring a bell.

"After we won the SEC championship in 1991 we said we've got to come up with a nickname. Well, I had remembered reading about John Tigert's descriptions of picking the site and he described it as a marshy area, a swampy depression. That's when we started focusing on The Swamp. Steve (Spurrier) liked the idea that a **swamp is where Gators** live and only Gators get out of the swamp alive. Now there were some people who didn't like it, but when we started promoting it, it took off like wildfire, so we started using it in the fall of 1992."

Thanks in large part to Florida's massive media exposure, brought on by the Gators' amazing success in the decade of the '90s, including a 30-game home winning streak, The Swamp gained a national reputation **as the loudest stadium** in the country. It lived up to that reputation numerous times in the '90s and continues to produce its deafening roar in the 21st century.

> " *We had talked about getting a nickname for the stadium because we thought it would help from an exposure standpoint. Everything we came up with was tacky. Nothing ever seemed to ring a bell.* "

As soon as the Gators race out through the south endzone tunnel, accompanied by the familiar "He-r-r-r-r-e-e-e-e Come The Gators" call, the focus of a trip to The Swamp moves squarely onto Florida Field and the game that will take place there. For many hours both before and after the deafening roar of those 90,000 plus fans reverberates throughout the stands, the essence of football weekends in Gainesville is played out at locations immediately surrounding The Swamp and for miles beyond. Call it a tradition, a ritual, **even an addiction,** but when it comes to tailgating, Florida football fans are among the nation's best at enjoying each other's company and having a grand time.

It's nearly impossible to try to peg an individual or group of fans as being representative of everything that makes tailgating at Gator football games so special. Yet if there is a poster child for the **art of tailgating** it has to be Stumpy Harris, a 1965 graduate of the University of Florida Law School.

Since starting to tailgate in 1966, the Harris entourage has expanded from a single car to a full-blown caravan of more than a dozen vehicles that has endearingly been labeled Stumpy's Gator Fleet. During the **"evolutionary process"** as Stumpy calls it, members of the fleet became so recognizable that many people thought they were actually owned by the University of Florida, even though every vehicle was purchased by Harris with the intention of being an important part of the tailgating experience.

While the "fleet" became a Gator game-day tradition, holding down a dozen parking spots in and next to the parking garage directly across from The Swamp, it all started with that single car top covered with food and drink in 1966.

"We went from the car to a pickup truck so we **could be true** tailgaters," Harris explained. "We'd cook steak after games, and we'd even use crystal and have a candelabra to make it classy."

Although he enrolled at UF in 1956, Harris stuck around Gainesville for more than a decade, graduating from law school and then teaching law for several years before **moving to Orlando** in 1969. He became a very successful attorney and with that success, and a growing family, the expansion of the tailgating experience became a natural process.

"As my family grew we really began to get involved with more equipment," Harris noted. "We maintained the pickup (which was painted orange and blue) to carry supplies, and then I got a van for out-of-town trips."

In the late '80s, Harris had a trio of **orange and blue canvas** pop-up tents made to house the ever-expanding parties that drew not only family members, but friends as well, to his site before and after games. There were loads of material to haul to each game, so Harris added a luggage trailer to the back of the pick-up truck. Then came the orange and blue van. After a few years, and especially after his kids went off to college, the workload became a bit too much.

> "
> We went from the car to a
> pickup truck so we could be true
> tailgaters. We'd cook steak
> after games, and we'd even use
> crystal and have a candelabra to
> "
> make it classy.

"There was so much material that you had to pack the trailer just a certain way to make it all fit," Harris noted. "I was working more than I wanted to on the front and back end, but we had a **rolling tailgate party** that we would use for road games. We had one road trip for couples each year and one trip for the boys and then we'd all come to the home games."

Harris was always trying to find a way to make the tailgating experience better, and the upgrade that was needed most was a bathroom. **So Stumpy made it happen.**

"We always had to go over to the O'Connell Center to go to the bathroom, so I decided to have a trailer built with a bathroom, a sink and a changing area. I got rid of the luggage trailer and we started travelling with the van, the truck and the bathroom trailer."

Again, the growth of his family dictated further expansion. With two kids and spouses, plus five grandchildren, Stumpy was in the market for something bigger and better to cart the entourage to Gainesville. He found a 1976 GMC motorhome and had the inside completely renovated. He took out the beds, used the space to install seating and **added five TVs** for the ultimate football-game viewing and partying experience. The fleet now included the pickup truck (known as The Mother Ship), the van, the bathroom vehicle (aka The Mother Lode) and his motor home. But there was still more to come.

"I bought a 1952 MG-TD, a real classic, and had it rebuilt and painted orange and blue," Harris said. "We named it Baby Gator. It wasn't convenient to bring it to Gainesville, but we brought it in an enclosed truck. Then we had the big trailer to cart the four Vespas (motorcycles), bicycles and everything else."

Lots of Gator fans are familiar with the various elements of Stumpy's fleet, but the vehicle that became the best known in the '80s was a Cadillac limousine, painted orange and blue, of course, with a big football helmet on its hood and speakers attached, **always ready to blare out** Gator songs and cheers. The car became so identified with the Gators that Harris donated it to the athletic department so it could use it for functions year-round.

There is no question about Harris's love for Gator football and all its trappings, but the tailgating extravagances revolve around being with family and friends.

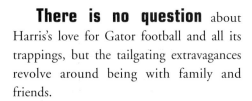

"It all turns around the idea that football is a time of the year when I'm with my family and friends," Harris acknowledged. "I see people I don't see anytime or anyplace. We have all kinds of people who stop by. The university president, United States senators, even (Florida) supreme court justices. **We are all the same.** Nobody gets down on a knee and kisses a ring. We always put out three huge coolers, one with Diet Coke, one with beer and one with other pop and water. We let people come in to use the bathroom. **We welcome anybody,** even opponents' fans, as long as they aren't mean spirited. We're just fans. It's all about family and friends."

And Stumpy Harris has lots of friends.
As a longtime Bull Gator member of Gator Boosters, Stumpy has been a vibrant part of the UF family for many years, and he's so well known throughout the state of Florida that a letter addressed to Stumpy Harris, Orlando, Florida, once arrived to him without problems. Ask somebody who Gordon H. Harris is, though, and most people would be clueless. That's Stumpy's given name, but it's used so rarely it sounds out of place to nearly everyone who knows him.

"I played football at Jacksonville Lee in ninth grade, and one day someone said I was as hard to move as a tree stump." Harris said of his nickname's origin. "I couldn't shake it, and I've taken it as a name of endearment ever since."

As if his legendary tailgating status wasn't enough, Stumpy also played an integral part in the development of the current Gator mascot.

"I told Charley Pell one of my pet peeves was the Pogo Gator, that he wasn't ferocious enough, that he didn't convey a winning tradition," Stumpy revealed. "I knew somebody at Disney, a shop foreman who made characters for Disney, and I asked him if he could build a prototype for a new Gator. It showed up in 1980 **as the new mascot,** which evolved into what we have now. The guy who did it made me swear I'd keep his secret until he passed away because he didn't want anybody at Disney to know about it. Then one year he came up to me and opened his trunk and asked what I would give him for the prototype. **He still had it.** He gave it to me and that's the Gator head that sits right on front of The Mother Lode."

> **"**
> *I knew somebody at Disney, and I asked him if he could build a prototype for a new Gator. It showed up in 1980 as the new mascot, which evolved into what* **"**
> *we have now.*

With his purchase of a 30-seat suite in the new Florida Field addition that opened in 2003, Stumpy Harris decided to cut back on the full-scale caravan approach to game day. He even put his **beloved Gator motor home** up for auction, with all proceeds from the sale donated to the UF athletic department. The tailgating entourage may be reduced somewhat, but the significance of those six Saturdays in Gainesville each fall hasn't ebbed one bit. **Just how important are they?** No friend or family member figures to make the unforgivable mistake of scheduling a wedding on the same day as a Gator football game.

"I don't go to weddings," Harris said sternly. "I can't sanction a union of genes for those who would think of doing it on a football weekend. Certain things are more important than that."

For Stumpy Harris, Gator football is one of those things.

There have been many arguments over the years about which game at The Swamp was the loudest ever in terms of a sustained level of high decibel noise. The game that seems to be mentioned more often than all others is the 1991 contest against Florida State. The 14-9 final score may not have lent itself to a **huge number of outbursts** after key offensive or defensive plays by the Gators, but because of the nature of the struggle between the two teams, every play seemed to build in significance as the game went on. Everybody seemed to sense that a single play could determine the final outcome. The game literally became enveloped by **a deafening roar** that continued for three hours, with only short lulls during TV **timeouts and programmed breaks** after each quarter.

At isolated moments in various games over the years, The Swamp has reached that same type of fevered pitch. And at every Gator home game since 1965, fans in attendance have been guaranteed at least one of those **defining moments** that send shivers through the body as the cheering and clapping volume reaches ear-ringing proportions. It may only last 10-12 seconds, but when the stadium public address **announcer calls out** "He-e-e-e-e-r-r-r-r-r-r-r-e Come The Gators," it is officially game time at The Swamp.

Jim Finch's call bringing the Gators out of the south endzone tunnel became so famous during the 37 years he produced it live that it became not only one of the most famous traditions in Florida Football history, but one of the most famous traditions in all of Southern college football.

The introduction of the players was actually in place when Finch took over as the stadium p.a. announcer in 1965, but it **didn't take him long** to make it his own signature call.

"It was there, but I added the stretch on it," Finch said in a 1989 interview for a feature in the Gator game day football program. "I dragged it out. I just threw in a few more e's and r's. I'm very proud of it. **It's a definite tradition."**

From 1965-2001, there were only two games that Finch didn't deliver his distinctive call. Once was because of an electrical failure just before the team came out on the field, and the other was when TBS, which was televising the SEC football game package, decided it wanted to try something different. The **Gators ended up losing** that game, and Finch was never allowed to miss the pregame call again.

Finch, who moved to Gainesville in 1962 to work for a radio station, had served as the play-by-play announcer for Gainesville High School football games for two years when Norm Carlson, UF's **sports information director,** called and offered him the stadium announcer's job.

> **"** *If you'll notice the timing, the fans are sitting there all pumped up waiting for the team to come back out on the field again. I got pumped up, too. When they come on the field, I let go and the fans* **"** *let go.*

"When Norm asked me if I'd do the P.A., I jumped at the chance," Finch said.

Over the years, Finch extended the "Here" portion of his introduction a few extra seconds, actually **stretching the entire call** out to 14 seconds on big-game days.

"Basically, I'm just like a regular fan," Finch said of the development of the introduction. "If you'll notice the timing, the fans are sitting there all pumped up waiting for the team to come back out on the field again. **I get pumped up, too.** When they come on the field, I let go and the fans let go."

"Other than him making it longer and longer over the years, he really didn't change it," his wife, Marion, said of the ritual. "Once in awhile he did it at home, just to **get ready for the season,** but otherwise he usually saved it for the games."

Finch was born in North Dakota and grew up in Minneapolis, where he lived a block from the University of Minnesota.

"When I was a kid, everybody would come walking by on Saturdays, **headed for football games,** and I could never afford to go to one," Finch said. "Now I get the best seat in the house—and get paid for sitting in it."

In addition to his introduction of the Gators, Finch had the game-long responsibility of delivering announcements to the fans in the stands, whether it be ads for Sea World, **requests for fans** to report to stadium locations, or for many years, before the fancy scoreboards were put into the stadium, providing scores of other football games around the SEC and the rest of the country.

Millions of Gator fans heard Finch's distinctive voice over the years, but only a small minority would have known him if they passed him walking down the street. He was a man of anonymity for most of his **announcing career,** but anyone who has been to a Gator game since 1965, will never forget the call he made famous. As a tribute to Finch, a tape of his introduction was used before games throughout the 2002 and 2003 seasons, and new public address announcer Jack O'Brien, who took over the rest of **Finch's announcing duties** during the 2002 season, was quite pleased to see Finch's traditional call still being used.

"I think it's **a tribute to Jim** and would like to see it continue," said O'Brien, who delivers the "Here Come The Gators" introduction when the **Gators return to the field** after halftime. "He (Finch) was an institution. I'm filling really big shoes."

On the night before game day, caravans of mobile homes make their way to familiar tailgating spots on campus and thousands of other fans fill up the hotel rooms around Gainesville and surrounding towns. Before those fans **awaken to start** their Saturday activities, and before they settle into their seats at The Swamp to watch their beloved Gators play football, a sizeable number of non-ticket holders spend many hours preparing the stadium, and its surrounding areas, for **an experience that extends** beyond the activity on the playing field.

While the plan for coordinating the more than 2,000 personnel who will work in and around The Swamp is put in place many months before the season-opening game, each game brings its own potential problems. A dozen key staff members from the University Athletic Association, headed up by athletic director Jeremy Foley, **meet for breakfast** at 6:30 a.m. on football Saturdays (6:00 a.m. if the game is set for a 12 noon regionally televised kick-off) to review assignments and unusual circumstances that **could arise during the day.** But before Foley and his troops start eating breakfast, preparations have already gotten underway over at The Swamp.

It's still a couple hours before the sun will rise on this Saturday morning in September, but the heat and humidity can already be felt around the stadium. As is so often the case, the game will be shown on national TV, and although fans are more comfortable when September games are played in the late afternoon or early evening, conference contracts with the networks, and the dollars that go with them, dictate the starting times for most contests. By 5:00 a.m., the most extensive logistical effort that will take place at the stadium this day is set to get underway. Trucks have arrived at The Swamp with the single most important item (other than a Gator victory) needed to **keep the 90,000 plus fans** comfortable during a steamy afternoon in the Florida sun—ice.

Lots of ice. How about 60 tons or 120,000 pounds of ice to be delivered to dozens of locations within the stadium? The bulk of the ice is used to cool down drinks in the **147 concession stands** throughout the stadium, but it also gets delivered to suites in the Touchdown Terrace and Bull Gator Deck, the President's Deck, the Champions Club, team locker rooms and for on-the-field use during the game. It takes **three to four hours** to unload the ice throughout the stadium, and the 5:00 a.m. start is necessary to ensure that food and drinks will have sufficient time to get cooled down before fans arrive. No matter **how hot it may get** on game day, running out of ice is not an option. A reserve of 12,000 pounds is kept on hand for emergency purposes.

Several hours after the icing process has begun, usually around 8:00 a.m., guards begin taking their places at the 19 parking lots on campus that are under the game-day supervision of the UAA. These lots are **set aside for various season** ticket holders, key university personnel and media represen- tatives, but represent only a small percentage of the more than **23,000 parking spaces** available on campus. Unlike other campuses around the Southeast, the majority of parking spaces at UF used to handle **game-day parking** are located away from the immediate area of the stadium.

Once the gates to Florida Field open 90 minutes before the scheduled kickoff time, some 375 ticket takers and ushers are in place to direct fans to their seats. Another 800 to 1,000 concession workers are also ready to **provide food and drinks** for the thousands of fans on hand. The number of drinks served varies according to the heat index before, during and even after the game with an average of 60,000 sold each Saturday. **The average breakdown** is some 30,000 sodas, 20,000 bottles of water and another 10,000 bottles of Gatorade, but on unusually warm days or for **an overflow crowd** attending the Tennessee game in September, upwards of 40,000 sodas, 30,000 bottles of water and 15,000 Gatorades have raised the drinks sold to the 85,000 mark.

Then, of course, there's food. Nine thousand hot dogs are sold each game along with 4,000 pretzels or 2,000 bags of peanuts and a matching number of boxes of popcorn. And beyond the standard concession-stand fare are **the specialty foods** that have become popular in recent years. More than $150,000 in revenue is generated each season from sales of cotton candy, pizza, seafood, nuts, bar-b-q, lemonade and ice cream products.

While the bulk of the personnel employed during game day deal with taking care of the hunger and thirst needs of the fans, hundreds of other workers provide important services to make sure the game-day **operations run smoothly** both inside and outside The Swamp.

Some 250 campus and Gainesville-area law enforcement officers are used to provide security at and around the stadium. All phases of security have taken on **added significance** since September 11, 2001.

"Since 9/11, stadium security has been bumped up to a higher level," explained Chip Howard, Florida's assistant athletic director for auxiliary services. "Now there are concrete barriers and metal bollards (thick metal posts) outside the stadium. We also use the **latest technology** so we can have the top security available."

Because of the many heat-related problems that occur at The Swamp, each game is staffed with 25 Alachua County Fire Department employees as well as a pair of emergency room doctors. Weather conditions are such an overriding concern on game days that a **south endzone maintenance** room is converted into a computer station used by a weather expert brought in to locate, and predict, potential weather-related problems before they reach The Swamp.

"The game against Ohio University (in 2002) was the first time we had to stop a game in more than 20 years," Howard noted. "Thanks to the computer program we **knew about the storm** before it arrived. We were able to monitor the lightning strikes within 15 seconds of their location. Once there was a strike within six miles of the stadium, we automatically stopped the game."

" Thanks to the computer program we knew about the storm before it arrived. We were able to monitor the lightning strikes within 15 seconds of their location. Once there was a strike within six miles of the stadium, we automatically stopped the game. "

While most kickoff times are dictated by the TV networks, research over the years has helped the UAA set starting times for those games that aren't televised live. Studies indicate that **the heat index,** a combination of the temperature and humidity, is generally at its lowest around 6:00 p.m. in the evening, a starting time that provides some relative comfort for the fans while still allowing enough time after the game for a majority of those who drove to the game to get back home at **a somewhat reasonable hour** of the night.

Once fans have cleared out of the stands, maintenance crews begin the clean-up process, getting The Swamp ready for that next wave of excitement. The state's largest team sports venue will be filled again soon with fans poised to welcome their heroes back through the south endzone tunnel for another day, or night, of **Fightin' Gator football.** The thousands of people who work to make the experience safe, enjoyable, and most of all, memorable, will also be there—well before the start to well after the finish of every game day at The Swamp.

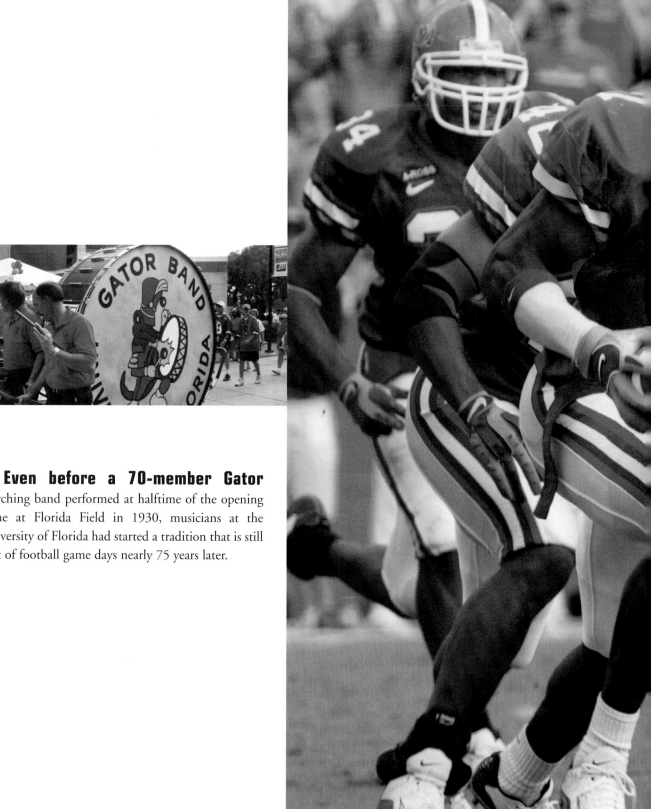

Even before a 70-member Gator
marching band performed at halftime of the opening
game at Florida Field in 1930, musicians at the
University of Florida had started a tradition that is still
part of football game days nearly 75 years later.

> **"**
> *We Are The Boys from old*
>
> *Florida, F-L-O-R-I-D-A...Where the*
>
> *girls are the fairest, the boys*
>
> *are the squarest of any old state*
>
> *down our way...We are all strong*
>
> *for old Florida down where the*
>
> *old Gators play. ...In all kinds of*
>
> *weather we'll all stick together*
> **"**
> *for F-L-O-R-I-D-A.*

There is no scene anywhere in college football, or all of college sports for that matter, that can match the **visual and emotional** impact of the one that takes place at the conclusion of the third quarter at every home football game in The Swamp. In a one-of-a-kind show of allegiance, fans sitting side by side put their arms around each other, even if they are strangers away from Florida Field, and begin to sway back in forth in unison while singing:

"We Are The Boys from old Florida, F-L-O-R-I-D-A...Where the girls are the fairest, the boys are the squarest of any old state down our way...We are all strong for old Florida down where the old Gators play...In all kinds of weather we'll all stick together for F-L-O-R-I-D-A."

The only people who don't move back and forth are the fans of the Gators' opponent, yet even they enjoy seeing the unabashed joy exuded by the Gator faithful during a ritual unique to Florida football. A ritual that had been established at UF many years before it **became a football** game-day tradition.

"We Are The Boys" was a popular dance song at fraternity dances and its first public rendition came in the 1920s at Gator Growl, the student-run pep rally that became part of Homecoming Weekend in 1925. Big-name comedians now serve as headliners for Gator Growl, which has always included songs, speakers and student skits, but in the 1920s and '30s the headline **event of Gator Growl** was the campus-wide boxing matches.

Before Florida Field was built in 1930, the ring for the boxing matches was placed in the northwest corner of Fleming Field, next to the stands. In the midst of one of the earliest Gator Growls, "We Are The Boys" was introduced in public for the first time. Students joining together to sway back and forth while singing the song became so popular that by the time Gator Growl and football games moved to Florida Field, the **tradition was already well entrenched.**

The tradition of playing "We Are The Boys" at the end of the third quarter is so popular that during a game in 2003, after the fans had finished singing and swaying, the officials decided time had not run out in the period and put several seconds back on the clock for another final play of the third quarter. After the play was over, the band struck up "We Are The Boys" a second time and **the fans were delighted** to repeat their part of the popular ritual.

Leading the fans in "We Are The Boys" may be the best-known stadium tradition performed by Florida's marching band, but there are numerous other activities that have made the band a tradition in its own right throughout Florida Field history.

That group of musicians known as the "Fightin' Gator Marching Band" in 1930, has grown to become a 300-member contingent that underwent a name change to "The Pride of The Sunshine" in 1975. While most fans are familiar with the band's activities inside the stadium, its pregame and postgame performances have become popular with fans as well.

Several hours before marching down North-South Drive on their way into The Swamp to take their seats in the lower corner of the north endzone, band members have their traditional 60-75 minute warmup session around the Gator statue on the Plaza of the Americas. For many years, the band warmed up in a room on campus, but as the band grew in size, **there wasn't enough space** for the percussion section so the decision was made to move outside for the pregame session. The move was a welcome one for fans, especially former band members, who have made it a habit to show up several hours before game time to **get revved up for the football game** while the band gets ready for its stadium show.

> **We try to keep our fans involved as much as possible. That's something I think we do better than other bands.**

After completing the warmup, the band begins its trek toward North-South Drive, where it will march past, and sometimes even through, thousands of fans who are making their way into the stadium. The march to the **north endzone** has been a "tradition" only since 1999, when the band was moved from its longtime stadium seating location near the **35-yard line in the east stands** to the north endzone.

Once inside the stadium, **The Pride of the Sunshine** tries to remain an integral part of the game atmosphere, both before and after its halftime show.

"We stay in the game and keep playing, especially between plays," band director Matt Sexton explained. "We try to **keep our fans involved** as much as possible. That's something I think we do better than other bands."

While there are a wide variety of songs that have become standard fare at Florida Field, no band-led cheer has become more popular than "Gator Jaws," which was developed by trombone player Adren Hance in the early '80s. In recent years, it has become the theme music for the scoreboard introduction used just prior to the Gators coming out of the south endzone tunnel onto the field at game time.

Based on the eerie music from the movie *Jaws* that signaled the looming appearance of a giant, man-eating shark, the Gator Jaws cheer is yet another visual thrill for fans as thousands join in raising and lowering their hands together in the shape of a jaw, this time a **ferocious gator's** rather than a carnivorous shark's.

The *Jaws* theme may have been creatively adapted for Gator football games, but it was Steve Spurrier's return to Florida in 1990 that sparked the re-enactment of a long-standing musical tradition that went out of vogue during the 1970s and '80s.

As a collegiate star in the mid-'60s, Spurrier had been part of the postgame tradition of players and fans joining together after games, win or lose, to sing the Alma Mater. As that rare head coach who was not only an alumnus of, but also deeply loved the school he coached at, Spurrier was insistent that having the team remain on the field after the game to sing the Alma Mater was important to foster school loyalty and **honor the University.** After those rare losses at home (only seven in Spurrier's 12 years as the Gator head coach), it may not have been easy to do, but the head ball coach and the vast majority of his players never failed to face the south endzone scoreboard as the words flashed by while **accompanied by The Pride of The Sunshine band:**

Florida, our Alma Mater...

Thy glorious name we praise..

All thy loyal sons and daughters...
A joyous song shall raise...

Where a palm and pine are blowing...
Where southern seas are flowing...

Shine forth thy noble Gothic walls...
Thy lovely vineclad halls...

'Neath the Orange and Blue victorious
our love shall never fail...

There's no other name so glorious...
All hail, Florida, hail.

After the Alma Mater has been played, another postgame musical highlight is only minutes away as the band files out of the north endzone. The drumline, which current band director Matt Sexton was a member of during his undergraduate days at UF, heads off to Turlington Plaza to perform FLAPS—the Florida Parade Sequence. **It's one last chance** for fans to enjoy the showmanship and musical skill of their school's marching band before they head off to a final round of tailgating, a fitting end to yet another **memorable day of sights and sounds** at The Swamp.

A combination of factors have come together over the years to turn Florida Field, **aka The Swamp,** from a somewhat noisy, difficult road venue for visiting teams to a very loud, if not the loudest, college football stadium in America.

Sheer numbers are important, of course, with the multiple expansions that have increased seating capacity from around 60,000 in 1980 to just more than 90,000 in 2003. The improved product on the field, as the Gators went from SEC-title wannabes to **full-fledged dominators** of the league in the '90s, not only insured sellout crowds but also brought **a raised level** of expectations, and in turn more game-day energy, to those in attendance. An overwhelming record of success on the home turf built upon itself to establish the aura that made national commentators label The Swamp the loudest **game-day spectacle** in all of college football.

Even with all of the above in place, there has also been another consistent catalyst helping to set everything in motion on the field. Many Gator fans have their own pregame rituals to get fired up before they head inside Ben Hill Griffin Stadium, but once they all gather **together in the stands** to encircle the playing field, there's a well-planned routine set in motion to create a single unit of enthusiasm, energy, emotion and most of all noise, that climaxes with the Gators running out of the south endzone tunnel to an ear-ringing, even deafening, wave of sound.

It all starts with Gator pregame. And Gator pregame starts with cheerleader-turned-stadium ringmaster Richard Johnston.

Johnston, who was a UF cheerleader in the late '70s and **returned to Gainesville** to lead the pregame ritual in 1984, believes The Swamp's pregame buildup is unique. It only takes about two minutes, but that 120 seconds is memorable.

"We've run the same format for about ten years with modifications here and there," Johnston explained. "We want to emphasize reaching that pinnacle at the right moment so The Swamp is ready to be as formidable a place and intimidating a place for Gator opponents as it can be. One thing that has never changed **since I began cheering** in the late '70s is that the Gator fans are constant. They have always been there backing their team, even when the successes on the field weren't there."

Back in the '70s, the pregame buildup ended with the team running out from the southeast corner of the endzone. It was the era of Doug's rug, when the Gators were **coached by Doug Dickey** and played on an artificial surface that made a hot day at Florida Field even hotter. Funding for cheerleaders was split between the University Athletic Association and Student Government, and there was no coordinated effort to create a standard pregame atmosphere.

When Charley Pell took over as head coach in 1979, the idea of upgrading the Gator program from top to bottom took hold. Johnston points to the 1980 home opener as a turning point in the process.

"We opened in Tampa and just killed California (41-14) and then we went to Atlanta and beat Georgia Tech. When we came home for that first game (against Mississippi State) it seemed like we just **connected with the crowd,** and it took off from there."

> **"**
> *We opened in Tampa and just killed Califonia (41-14) and then we went to Atlanta and beat Georgia Tech. When we came home for that first game (against Mississippi State) it seemed like we just connected with the crowd, and it took off* **"** *from there.*

Among the traditions already in place was the passing up of students, a popular exercise that took place several times a game when students in the lower east stands would pass a student up through the crowd until he or she was **several dozen rows** higher in the stands than they started. UF officials brought the tradition to a halt after some creative students **dressed up a mannequin** as a cheerleader, passed it all the way to the top of the East Stands, before students on the top row threw the mannequin over the wall and out of the stadium to the horror of the alumni-packed West Stands.

There was also the short-lived fame of Mr. Banana, a student dressed as a banana who would dance around to the chant of "Go bananas, go-go bananas." And as Johnston **remembered fondly,** after the rendition of "We Are The Boys" was finished before the start of the fourth quarter, students would take the plastic lids from their soda cups and **wing them onto the field** like they were Frisbees as cheerleaders tried to catch as many as possible in their megaphones. But plenty of other traditions have survived over the years.

According to Johnston, the three most important elements of the pregame ritual are Mr. Two Bits, the band and the "Here Come The Gators" chant that brings the players onto the field.

"If I have a theory of cheerleading it's that we really weren't just supposed to entertain or just yell, but we were supposed to connect the crowd to the field," said Johnston, a UF law school graduate who currently practices law in Ft. Myers. "That's happened **more and more over the years.** So you have to bring those three things together and then you also want to build it to that pitch so when the guys come out of the tunnel it's an explosion of sound and color and noise and just epitomizes The Swamp."

All of those elements weren't in place when Johnston returned to take charge of the pregame in 1984 after assistant athletic director Richard Giannini decided **something was missing** from the lead up to the kickoff of each home game.

"When I started again in '84, it surprised me that George (Edmondson, Mr. Two Bits), who was so recognizable and had such a signature cheer, wasn't part of pregame. I called him and asked him why he never did pregame and he said **nobody ever asked him.** So I asked him. I know it sounds simple, but he's such a huge tradition from the grassroots up."

"The second thing was you had to tie in with the band. The band has that wonderful spell out (of the word Gators). And spell out, for me, has to be one of the most exciting moments in pregame. I get to pull the switch on 90,000 people every year. When you get in the middle of it and say give me a "G" and everybody yells it out, well that's the tie in with the crowd. Then with **Gator Jaws** too, the band has been constantly innovative in new marches and new ideas. There was a time back in the '70s when the band and the cheerleaders didn't get along as well as they could and that's all changed now.

"It's been taking these singular elements and weaving them together, and over the years it has gotten more and more tight on time. We have more traditions, we're trying to do more in pregame. Every Gator has **their own pregame ritual** and many of them are unique, but they all end up at the stadium, some in time for pregame, and so most of the traditions we focus on are old cheers because we only have time for so much."

> **"**
> *Every Gator has their own pregame ritual and many of them are unique, but they all end up at the stadium, some in time for pregame, and so most of the traditions we focus on are old cheers because we only have* **""** *time for so much.*

Among the standard cheers that have stood the test of time are "Let's Go Gators," "Orange and Blue," "Here We Go Gators," and of course "Two-Bits." Add the chant of "Gator Bait" when the opponent comes out on the field and the fans doing the **Gator Chomp to the theme** from the movie *Jaws*, and there is a ready list of cheers to keep every-one busy both before and during the game. But while the play on the field generally dictates how loud the fans get at any moment during the game, it is still guaranteed that if the pregame ritual is timed out just right, one of the loudest roars of any gameday will take place **at the precise moment** the Gators pour out of the south endzone tunnel.

"My goal is to have the crowd just absolutely screaming when you hear that da-da, da-da, with the Gator Jaws video starting, if I can have them on their feet when that thing starts about five or ten seconds into the video when they say 'The Swamp, nobody except the Gators get out alive', and the 'Her-e-e-e-e Comes The Gators' rolls off, and the flags are waving and the fight song is playing..., well, I'm the **luckiest guy on Earth** six times a year. It is absolutely like a Saturn 5 (rocket) going off down there. It's hard to describe."

The most recognizable person at Gator football games isn't the head coach or a player. In fact, he isn't even a University of Florida graduate. Yet when George Edmondson runs onto Florida Field while the team is getting last-minute instructions in the locker room, he is the one person in the entire stadium who can draw **a tumultuous roar** from thousands of Gator faithful, silence the throng with a wave of his hand and then bring the crowd to another crescendo moments later.

He's been doing it for more than 50 years and very little of his brief, but unforgettable routine has changed over the decades. George Edmondson is **Mr. Two Bits.** And the tradition he started on September 24, 1949, at the season opener between The Citadel and Florida is without a doubt the single most enduring tradition in the nearly century-old history of Gator football.

More than 350 football games have been played at Florida Field since the inaugural contest against Alabama in 1930. Nearly 300 of them have been played since that fall day in 1949 when George Edmondson traveled with a friend from his home in Tampa to see his alma mater (The Citadel) take on the Gators. Edmondson **has missed only three** home games in the years since that first trip to Florida Field, the only times he hasn't led Gator fans in the two-bits cheer.

Ironically, it was booing that got him to start cheering for the Gators.

"I couldn't believe it when I heard everybody booing the team when it ran out on the field," Edmondson said of the 1949 team coached by Raymond "Bear" Wolf. "I felt bad for them. The kids were trying hard, but the fans didn't seem to care about that. I told the people around us that every time they (the players) **make a mistake let's cheer** for them. Well when I did it, everybody thought we were drunk."

After four lousy seasons under Wolf (the Gators compiled a 13-24-2 record during his tenure), Bob Woodruff was hired in 1950 to revive Florida's football fortunes. With the first of what would become **five Florida Field expansions** set to be completed for the 1950 season opener, a new enthusiasm figured to take hold of the Gator football program. But according to Edmondson, it just didn't happen.

"Things didn't change much right away, but I started doing the cheer again for all the home games," he noted. "We didn't do much for a couple years (5-5 seasons in both 1950 and '51) but then in 1952 **we went to the Gator Bowl** and won and that seemed to get people real excited."

> " I felt bad for them. The kids were trying hard, but the fans didn't seem to care about that. I told the people around us that every time they (the players) make a mistake let's cheer for them. Well when I did it, everybody thought we were drunk. "

That 14-13 win over Tulsa completed a highly successful 8-3 season and Edmondson and most other Gator fans figured things would only get better for the program. By now, the fans were starting to get used **to the two-bits routine** and Edmondson was ready to upgrade his performances.

"I got myself a little sign and I tooted a bugle to let people know I was there," Mr. Two Bits explained. "After a while the bugle got cumbersome so I got a whistle instead."

Mr. Two Bits led his cheer from row 83 in the newly expanded stadium, but after games were over, fans from other sections would come up and ask him to lead their sections in the cheer. He thought it was **a great idea and started to go** from section to section during the games.

What had started as one man's effort to offset negative fans in 1949 had turned into a full-blown tradition by the time Ray Graves's teams of the '60s started winning big on a regular basis. And the amazing thing was that **such a simplistic** cheer—Two bits, four bits, six bits, a dollar, all for the Gators, stand up and holler!—would become the single most popular rallying cry associated with Florida football.

"I lived near (Tampa) Plant high school back in the '30s and '40s and their football cheerleaders would always do the two-bits cheer," Edmondson said of his early association with his namesake. "I wanted to **get the fans involved,** and the cheer was quick, short, spontaneous and everybody knew it. I can hold up the sign and I don't have to do much hollering for it. If I had to yell every time I led the cheer, I would have lost my voice."

> **"** *I wanted to get the fans involved and the cheer was quick, short, spontaneous and everybody knew it. I can hold up the sign and I don't have to do much hollering for it. If I had to yell every time I led the cheer, I would have lost my voice.* **"**

But if people think George Edmondson has been showing up at Florida Field for 55 years just so he can lead the fans in cheers, well think again.

"I go to see the football game," he explained. "I hurry from place to place during time-outs on the field so I won't interfere with the game or miss the action. I try to keep myself at the other end of the field from **where the action is** and no lower than row 20 in the stands. I'm very careful with my whistle."

While the fans in the sections where Mr. Two Bits appears always seem surprised, and very excited, when he shows up to lead his cheer, he carefully plans his route through the stadium before he embarks on **his game-day ritual.** Before moving his seats from the east stands to the Touchdown Terrace a few years ago, Mr. Two Bits made his way from Section 12 on toward the north endzone on a route that included 10 to 12 stops per game. It wasn't until the mid-'70s that he started to include the student section in the east stands on his route.

"Students would see me after games and ask me why I didn't come over to their side," Mr. Two Bits said. "I figured since the students were always standing up and cheering and hollering, they didn't need me over there. But they wanted me, so I started going over. There was **always pandemonium** over there because they always wanted to take pictures with me or get autographs. It was great that they wanted me there, so I went."

It's no great surprise that fans all over the stadium want a picture with Mr. Two Bits. His uniform of a yellow long sleeve dress shirt, **Gator tie** and black-and-white saddle shoes, can be spotted easily even if he is in a section across the stadium from where you're sitting. The outfit has become so recognizable that when **Albert The Alligator** wears it at Gator basketball games everybody knows it's time for the obligatory two-bits cheer.

> **"**
> *I figured since the students were always standing up and cheering and hollering, they didn't need me over there. But they wanted me, so I started going* **"**
> *over there.*

"Back in the early days the ladies wore dresses and hose to the games and guys wore ties and coats. It was a lot more formal affair. I wore a yellow shirt because **it went with my Gator tie** and blue blazer," Mr. Two Bits explained.

"When it started getting more relaxed at the games I kept wearing the yellow shirt. Somebody suggested wearing an orange shirt, but then I wouldn't stand out from the crowd so I stayed with the yellow one."

As it turned out, the fashion statement became important for Mr. Two Bits to be able to maintain his **game-long cheering routine.**

"The early games in September get really hot," he noted. "My shirt would get completely soaked and then I noticed that **the wet shirt kept me cool** and comfortable when I was running around."

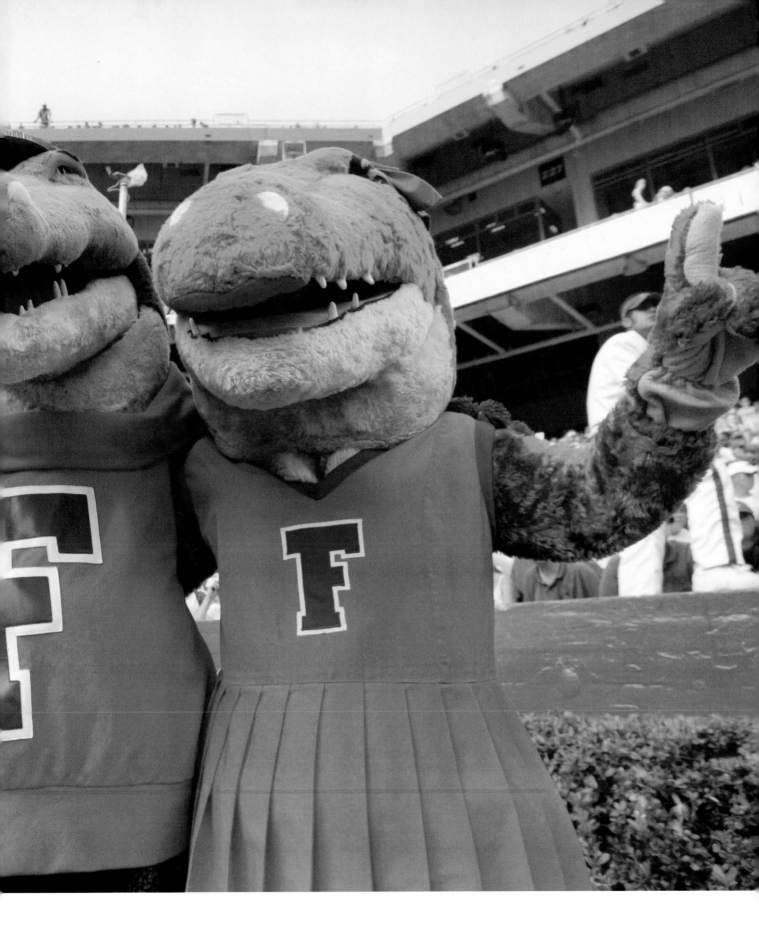

But even more famous than the yellow shirt and Gator tie are the black and white shoes that serve as a throwback to the '50s. They went out of style decades ago so Mr. Two Bits has had to search far and wide to be able to **keep a pair on his feet since 1949.**

"I wore those black and white bee bops because they had rubber soles and a good grip. I wore out a lot of those. I couldn't find the shoes after a while and then one time I saw them in the window of a women's shoe shop. I went in and asked for the biggest size they had and since I have a small foot I found some that fit. **I wore ladies' shoes** for two or three years before they wore out. Then I switched to golf shoes without the spikes. I've been using them and they've been very serviceable."

Mr. Two Bits had worn out a lot of shoes by the time he announced his retirement on November 15, 1998, after leading a couple generations of Gator fans through 50 years of cheers. But what was supposed to be **retirement has instead** become only a cutback in the number of cheers per game. Gator fans just wouldn't let him quit.

"All I got was static from people that I can't retire," the 82-year-old Edmondson noted in 2004. "I guess if Michael Jordan can come out of retirement so can I. I'm not quite as active as I used to be. We **changed our seats** to the Touchdown Terrace, and it used a lot of time getting up and down the elevators. Now that we're in the Champions Club, getting to the stands to lead cheers is cumbersome."

> **"**
> *When I blow my whistle and wave my hand and there's almost an eerie silence from all those fans.... and then there's that tremendous sound coming from all around me when I start two-bits.* **"**
> *It's just unbelievable.*

Still, as long as Mr. Two Bits keeps attending games at The Swamp, and considering how remarkably fit he is for his age, that could be for many years to come, **he has no plans to stop** leading his cheer.

"Some of my friends say I get hot and red in the face when I'm out there and that I'm going to have a heart attack," Edmondson said. "And I say to them, **'Can you think of any better place for it to happen?'**

"When I stand out in the middle of the field before a game **it's a tremendous feeling,"** he adds. "When I blow my whistle and wave my hand and there's almost an eerie silence from all those fans.... and then **there's that tremendous sound** coming from all around me when I start two-bits. It's just unbelievable."

Mr. Two Bits is an irreplaceable icon, even if there are would be replacements who want his "job" when he's gone.

"People call and they want to take my place," Edmondson noted. "But nobody can take my place. It's not going to be the same. There was one Babe Ruth and one Michael Jordan. There's only going to be **one Mr. Two Bits.**

"Some years back Hugh Culverhouse (the former owner of the Tampa Bay Buccaneers of the NFL) wanted me to come and work for him at the Bucs games. I was honored that he was interested, but I told him that what I do for the Gators is from the heart. If I ever **did it for the purpose** of making money it wouldn't be right...I guess I could've been another San Diego Chicken and my wife could've lived the life of luxury she deserves."

Mr. Two Bits never sold out, and in staying true to his Gator heart, he has created a rich Gator tradition like none other in college football. And a lifetime of memories that **will live on long** after his cheering stops.